IMAGES
OF BALI

PHOTOS BY HEINZ VON HOLZEN

Marshall Cavendish
Editions

© 2014 Marshall Cavendish International (Asia) Private Limited
Reprinted 2016

Published by Marshall Cavendish Editions
An imprint of Marshall Cavendish International
1 New Industrial Road, Singapore 536196

Editor: Stephanie Yeo
Design: Bernard Go Kwang Meng
Photographs: Heinz von Holzen

Other Marshall Cavendish Offices:
Marshall Cavendish Corporation. 99 White Plains Road, Tarrytown NY 10591-9001, USA ·
Marshall Cavendish International (Thailand) Co Ltd. 253 Asoke, 12th Flr, Sukhumvit 21 Road, Klongtoey Nua, Wattana, Bangkok 10110, Thailand · Marshall Cavendish (Malaysia) Sdn Bhd, Times Subang, Lot 46, Subang Hi-Tech Industrial Park, Batu Tiga, 40000 Shah Alam, Selangor Darul Ehsan, Malaysia.

Marshall Cavendish is a trademark of Times Publishing Limited

National Library Board, Singapore Cataloguing-in-Publication Data

Holzen, Heinz von, photographer.
Images of Bali / photos by Heinz von Holzen. – Singapore : Marshall Cavendish Editions, 2014.
pages cm
ISBN : 978-981-4516-07-5 (paperback)

1. Bali Island (Indonesia) – Pictorial works. 2. Bali Island (Indonesia) – Social life and customs – Pictorial works. I. Title.

DS647.B2
915.9862 — dc23   OCN 874104175

Printed in Singapore by Colorscan Print Co. Pte Ltd

IMAGES OF BALI

CONTENTS

01

INTRODUCTION

Widely regarded as Indonesia's most popular tourist destination, the idyllic island of Bali is beloved for its beautiful beaches and rugged mountains, rich traditions and friendly locals, as well as its robust arts and cultural scene.

BEGUILING BALI

One of more than 17,000 islands in the Indonesian archipelago, Bali lies to the east of Java at the westernmost end of the Lesser Sunda Islands, most of which are part of Indonesia. It is the country's smallest province with a population of over 4 million people, and is home to most of the country's Hindu minority.

Despite encompassing a small land area of just over 5,000 square kilometres, Bali's picturesque beauty knows no end. Its diverse landscape of vast sandy beaches, rugged coastlines, lush rice terraces, volcanic hillsides and mountains provide an alluring backdrop to its deeply spiritual and vibrant culture.

02

PEOPLE & CULTURE

Although deservingly celebrated as a tropical paradise, the essence of Bali is embodied in its warm, generous people and their colourful ceremonies, rich traditions and unique culture.

BALINESE HINDUISM

Balinese culture is strongly influenced by Indian, Chinese and particularly Hindu culture, with a unique blend of Hinduism and ancient mysticism. Nearly every aspect of Balinese life is suffused with religion, from the ubiquitous leaf trays (*canang sari*) placed in every home and temple in offering to the gods, to the sculptures of deities and guardians adorning temples and courtyards.

An important Hindu ritual in Bali is the tooth filing ceremony, a rite of passage into adulthood where one's teeth are smoothened in a symbolic gesture of ridding oneself of evil such as greed, anger and jealousy.

CANANG SARI

These tiny trays of offerings are made from palm leaves woven into baskets and filled with a range of items from flowers to betel nuts and glutinous rice. Balinese Hindus use *canang saris* in daily offerings to thank their primary deity, Sang Hyang Widhi Wasa, in praise and prayer.

NYEPI

Also known as the Hindu New Year, Nyepi is celebrated as a day of silence, during which all activities and business on the island come to a standstill. Locals and visitors alike observe complete inactivity for 24 hours from sunrise – the streets are deserted and even Bali's international airport closes for the day.

On the eve of Nyepi, colourful demon-like sculptures known as *ogoh-ogoh* are paraded through the streets in a traditional ceremony and offered gifts of food and flowers. The *ogoh-ogoh* are later burnt to symbolise the purging of evil spirits for the coming year.

TEMPLES & SHRINES

The *pura* (Balinese for 'temple') are inseparable from the religious rituals of Bali's Hindu faithful and are the most ubiquitous architectural structures on the island. Every home has its own shrine and each rice field has a shrine dedicated to Dewi Sri, the goddess of rice. Bali's largest and most important temple is the Mother Temple of Besakih on Mount Agung, the island's tallest mountain.

Left: Pura Pulaki in West Bali

Right: Pura Besakih (top) and Pura Ulun Danu Batur near Mount Batur (bottom)

The majestic Pura Geger at Geger Beach.

BALI AGA

The island's original natives, the Bali Aga ('mountain Balinese') – or Bali Mula ('original Balinese'), as they are often known – remain untouched by time and practise a conservative way of life that pre-dates modern civilisation. They live primarily in isolated mountainous areas, particularly in two main villages in eastern Bali, Tenganan and Trunyan.

TENGANAN

Although the Bali Aga generally discourage contact with outsiders, Tenganan has recently opened its doors to tourism and is renowned for its *geringsing* – traditional textiles that feature an intricate double ikat weaving technique.

TRUNYAN

This small Bali Aga village sits at the foot of Mount Abang on the eastern shore of Lake Batur. In stark contrast to Hindu funeral rites, the Truyanese do not cremate their dead but instead place the bodies in a bamboo cage under a giant, centuries-old banyan tree within their village grounds. When only the skeletons remain, the skulls are placed on a stepped stone altar.

View of Mount Batur overlooking Lake Batur and Trunyan village.

View of Trunyan village from Mount Abang.

The skulls of Truyanese dead are placed on a stepped stone altar within the village, making for a truly macabre sight.

ARTISTIC BALI

Artistic traditions are deeply immersed in Balinese culture. Encompassing a wide range of performing arts from dance to percussion orchestra music, and from traditional painters and sculptors in Ubud to contemporary art galleries in Seminyak, the island's multi-faceted arts culture is truly a feast for the senses.

Balinese dancers don a black and white checkered cloth, the *saput poleng*, as part of their costume. This sacred cloth is an integral part of the island's religious customs and is used everywhere from clothing to being wrapped around trees and fitted on statues and other decorations.

ART & CRAFT

Bali's vibrant art and craftwork
industry is a major draw for tourism,
boasting a diverse selection from
paintings to sculptures and textiles,
as well as intricate woodwork, stone
carvings and silverware.

BALINESE DANCE

The Balinese people's ancient dance tradition is an integral part of their religious and artistic expression. These visual and dramatic performances often draw from Hindu epics such as the *Mahabarata* and the *Ramayana*, and include popular dances such as the *kecak*, *legong* and *barong*.

KECAK

The *kecak*, or '*Ramayana* monkey chant' as it is also known, is a popular spiritual performance with up to 250 bare-chested male dancers chanting while rhythmically swaying their bodies and arms. They sit in in circles around the main performers, who dramatise an epic battle from the *Ramayana* while often in a trance.

LEGONG

This quintessential Balinese dance features just three performers; often two young females (known as *legong*) and their attendant. A graceful dance characterised by complicated footwork, intricate finger movements and expressive gestures, *legong* is often accompanied by a traditional *gamelan* orchestra, which features instruments such as bamboo flutes, xylophones and drums.

BARONG

One of the island's most visually spectacular performances, the *barong* – or 'lion dance' – depicts the eternal struggle between good and evil, as represented by the mythological lion-like Barong, the king of protector spirits, and his enemy Rangda, the demon queen.

WAYANG KULIT & GAMELAN

Shadow puppet theatre is a perennial favourite in Indonesia and is particularly popular in Java and Bali. '*Wayang*' means 'shadow' or 'ghost' in Javanese, while '*kulit*' (which means 'skin') refers to the thin leather sheets used to make the puppets. The shadows of these puppets are cast on a cotton or linen screen and a puppet master known as a *dalang* narrates the story, which often draws from Hindu epics such as the *Mahabarata* and the *Ramayana*.

03

LOCALES

Bali's diverse locales make it a popular tourist destination. Be it tranquil beach resorts or vibrant surf paradises, and from historical attractions to bustling cultural centres and gastronomic havens, the enigmatic island has something for everyone.

UBUD

Located in central Bali amid lush rice paddy fields and steep ravines, Ubud blends both rustic tradition and modern luxury as the island's main arts, cultural and spiritual centre. Traditional art galleries and ancient temple ruins sit near lavish boutique hotels, tranquil yoga retreats and spa resorts, and the sacred Ubud Monkey Forest is a stone's throw away for visitors seeking to unwind and commune with nature.

Ubud is renowned for its numerous temples and verdant rice terraces and is a popular location for a relaxing spiritual getaway.

SEMINYAK

The shopping and gastronomic haven of Seminyak is a bustling beach town filled with fashionable restaurants and nightspots, as well as upmarket commercial strips featuring quaint craft shops and designer boutiques. Unofficially known as the 'spa capital' of Bali, Seminyak is also famous for its grand hotels and beachside villas that offer the ultimate luxury experience.

KUTA

Bali's vibrant beach resort and surf paradise is the island's entertainment central and beloved by many for its long sandy beach, numerous restaurants and *warungs* (local shops or cafes), street markets, energetic nightlife and wide variety of accommodation to suit every pocket. Majestic mountains and cliffs frame the coast, lending to the jagged landscape and awe-inspiring views. Despite the bustle of activity, most of Kuta retains its charm as a fishing village, with the locals remaining largely unaffected by the surge in visitor numbers.

Locals and visitors throng the vibrant street markets in Kuta for the day's freshest produce.

NUSA DUA

Luxury resorts, pristine white sand and clear turquoise waters make this high-end beach enclave a perennial favourite with visitors, who gather on the southeastern side of the peninsula for plenty of sun, surfing and spas. Nusa Dua – which means 'two islands' in Balinese – is also home to Bali's most popular golf course and one of the island's best museums.

JIMBARAN

Any visit to Bali is incomplete without a trip to Jimbaran in the south. Once a backwater with a tiny fishing village and market, the bay is now home to several upmarket resorts and popular seafood restaurants overlooking the beach. These offer a picturesque view of the sunset in the evenings, and are a perfect spot to unwind at after a day of sightseeing.

Local vendors hawk their wares at
Jimbaran's busy street markets.

SANUR

One of the first resort beaches on Bali, the upscale resort area of Sanur on the eastern coast is a quiet, relaxed alternative to the excitement of Kuta. It boasts a growing number of popular hotels and villas, as well as a good mix of restaurants and bars, and is a good spot to try kitesurfing or canoeing due to its prime location near several breakwaters and a coral reef.

BUKIT PENINSULA

This large limestone peninsula at the southernmost tip of Bali is famous for the sea temple perched on a cliff, Pura Luhur Ulu Watu, which boasts jaw-dropping views of the surrounding ocean. The Bukit – as it is commonly known – also encompasses Balangan beach, one of the island's best beaches, and several top surfing locations in Bali.

Possibly Bali's most famous temple, Pura Ulu Watu is one of nine key directional temples intended to protect the island from evil spirits. Often awash with tourists and throngs of pickpocketing monkeys, the architectural wonder is constructed out of black coral rock and features well-preserved intricate carvings despite its exposure to the elements.

TANAH LOT

A renowned rock formation just off the coast of Bali, Tanah Lot is
home to Pura Tanah Lot, a venerated pilgrimage temple and an
important element of Balinese mythology and spiritualism. Extremely
popular for its picture-perfect sunsets and cultural exoticism,
the area is often crowded with visitors, particularly in the late
afternoons when the best photography spots are prime property.

DENPASAR

While most visitors tend to enter Bali via the Ngurah Rai International Airport in Denpasar and move on to other areas, the island's capital and most populated city is a growing commerce and cultural hub with shopping malls and markets, as well as several temples, palaces and museums. Local vendors ply their trade at the various traditional markets, hawking everything from fresh produce and livestock to kitchenware and handicraft.

CANDI DASA

A popular tourist stop in eastern Bali, Candi Dasa is a quiet coastal town on the edge of a freshwater lagoon with good diving and snorkelling options. Its laidback, almost sedate atmosphere and strategic location make it a good base from which to explore the surrounding region, particularly the scenic foothills of Mount Agung and Tenganan village, where the reclusive Bali Aga reside just several kilometres inland.

AMED

This cluster of small fishing villages in northeast Bali is a throwback to the days of yore. The locals retain a traditional lifestyle and rely primarily on fishing and salt production from seawater as a means of subsistence. Tourism in Amed has increased in recent years, and this once hidden gem is now well known for its natural beauty that stretches along the coast and as an excellent diving and snorkelling location.

Salt production is a declining but important industry in Amed. Sea water is poured into large open drying pans and left to dry, allowing salt crystals to form.

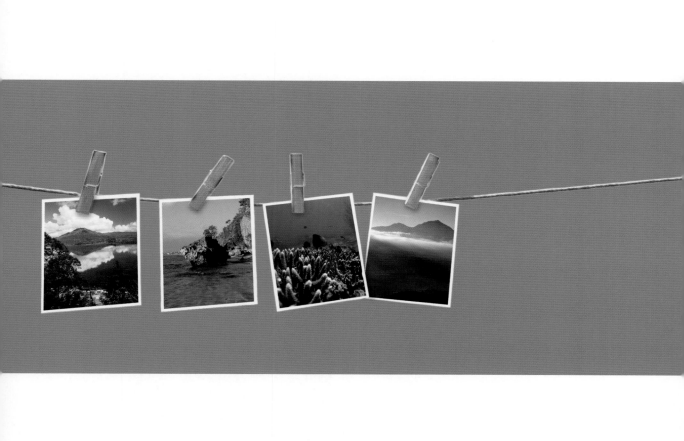

04

NATURE

Bali's abundant natural beauty makes it a true nature-lover's paradise. The island is surrounded by beautiful coral reefs and endless beaches and crashing waves envelope most of its shores. Away from the coast, verdant forests and terraced rice paddy fields form a lush backdrop to the island's majestic mountains and active volcanoes.

MOUNTAINS & VOLCANOES

Bali's towering mountain ranges and volcanic peaks dominate much of its landscape and significantly influence the island's climate and ecology. These majestic ranges stretch from the centre of the island to the east, and imbue the land with exceptional fertility, high rainfall and irrigation that support Bali's extremely productive agricultural industry.

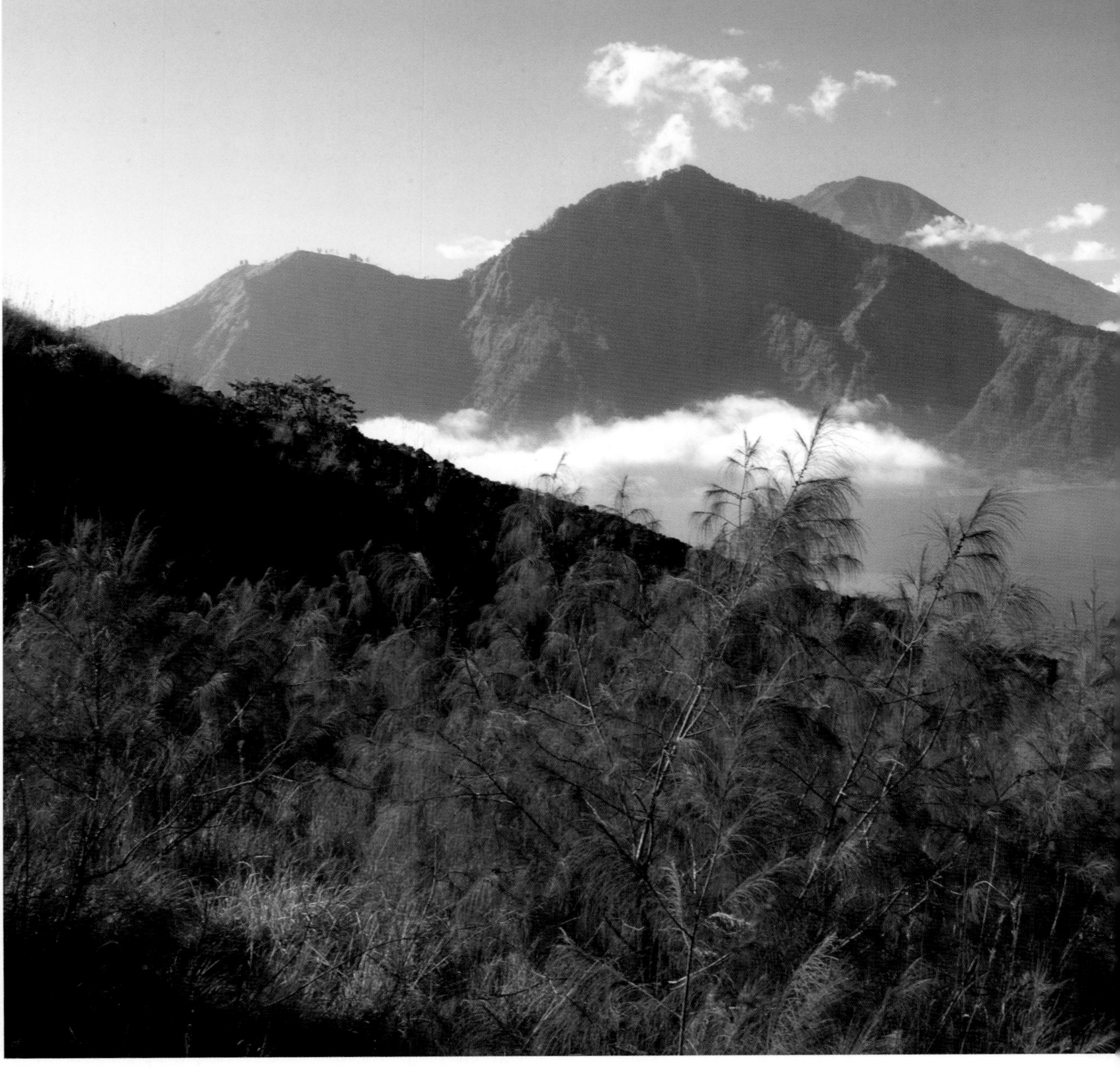

MOUNT AGUNG

The imposing Mount Agung (or Gunung Agung) is the island's highest point at over 3,000 metres above sea level, dominating the landscape in east Bali. Revered by locals as the sacred abode of the gods, this active volcano has not erupted since 1963 and is home to Pura Besakih, the 'Mother Temple' of Bali. Perched high up on the slope of Mount Agung, Pura Besakih comprises more than 20 separate temples and shrines, several dating back to the 14th century. As almost every shrine celebrates a yearly anniversary, at least 70 festivals are held at the complex every year.

MOUNT BATUR

This permanently smouldering active volcano in northeastern Bali overlooks the town of Kintamani and its serene crater lake within the vast caldera, Lake Batur. Mount Batur's last eruption was in 1994, and remnants of the black lava can still be seen nearby. One of Bali's most beloved temples, Pura Ulun Danu Batur, sits on the rim of the caldera, and is dedicated to the goddess of the lake, Dewi Danu.

The active volcano Mount Batur sits at the centre of two concentric calderas, one of which contains Lake Batur, the largest crater lake in Bali.

MOUNT BATUKARU

Unlike Mount Batur, Bali's second-highest volcano is less popular with mountain climbers due to its dense forests and restricted views. At over 2,000 kilometres above sea level, Mount Batukaru – which translates to 'coconut shell mountain' in Balinese – towers over centuries-old rice paddy fields, quaint villages and temples in nearby Bedugul and Jatiluwih. Another of the island's nine sacred directional temples, Pura Luhur Batukaru, sits on the volcano's southern slope amidst lush tropical rainforest.

RICE PADDY FIELDS

Rice cultivation is a vital component of Balinese life, from its agricultural economy to its food culture and even to religion. Indonesia is the world's seventh largest rice importer and has an estimated seventh highest per capita rice consumption rate in the world. Lush, verdant rice fields are thus the dominant agricultural feature of Bali, often in the form of dramatic sculpted terraces. These majestic emerald steps offer some of the island's best photo opportunities, and can be found in numerous locales, including Ubud, Pupuan in western Bali and Jatiluwih in the north.

BEACHES

Bali is renowned for its legendary beaches,
year-round diving spots and excellent waves
for surfing, with much of its coastline fringed
by soft, sandy beaches and surrounded by
turquoise waters and coral reefs. Particularly
enticing are the ever-popular stretches in Kuta,
Ulu Watu and Nusa Dua, which offer everyone
from thrill-seeking surfers to sun-kissed revellers
the perfect tropical paradise.

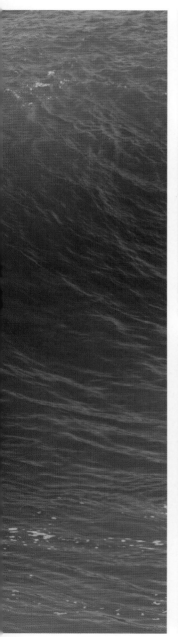

WEST BALI NATIONAL PARK

Bali's only national park is located in the northwestern tip of the island, encompassing various habitats over 190 square kilometres of land and sea, and a further 580 square kilometres of protected highland reserve in the east. The park is home to over 160 species of flora and fauna, including the Banteng, a species of Southeast Asian wild cattle, and the critically endangered Bali Myna.

FISHING

Despite the boom in tourism, Bali's economy remains largely agrarian and fishing is the primary occupation of many locals who live along the coast. Fish is a major source of protein for many Balinese as it is relatively affordable, easily caught and readily available in the markets, and many traditional fishing villages still exist in Amed and Padang Bai on the east coast.

TURTLE CONSERVATION

Still considered a delicacy in Bali, marine turtles are now under threat of extinction as a result of over-fishing and the plundering of their nests for egg consumption. Greater awareness about turtle conservation in recent years has led to a number of initiatives to save the endangered species. With the help of conservation teams and nature lovers, turtle eggs are collected from the markets and placed into safe hatching grounds and hatched under ideal conditions. The hatchlings are nurtured for a few weeks before being released back into the sea. Sick turtles are also given refuge and nursed back to health.

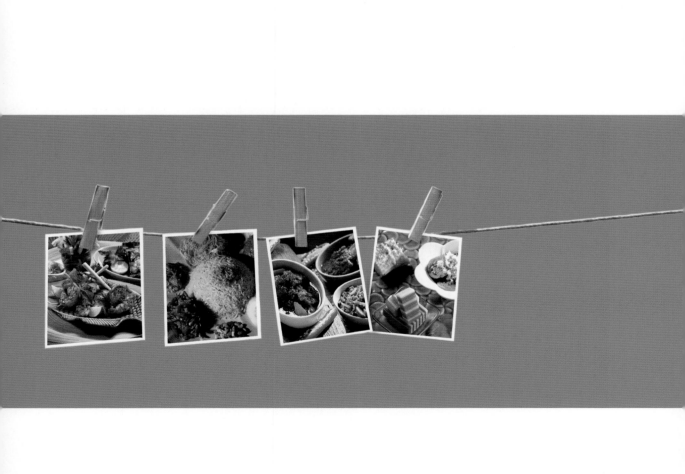

05

FOOD

Simple, inexpensive and unpretentious, Balinese cuisine is nonetheless full of flavour and tradition. Be it a *nasi padang* lunch at a local *warung* (cafe), local snacks from a street vendor or a meal at one of Jimbaran's famous grilled seafood restaurants, Bali's extensive food offerings are certain to whet one's appetite.

LOCAL MARKETS

There is no other place that captures the local colour, buzz and atmosphere of Bali as well as the markets peppered throughout the island. These local markets are filled with everything the island has to offer, from fresh produce such as meat, poultry, seafood and spices to essential Balinese cooking utensils, and most are in full swing from the early hours of the morning. These busy and vibrant markets are the centres of social life and offer an authentic glimpse into everyday Balinese life.

GRILLED SEAFOOD

Bali is famous for its grilled (*bakar*) seafood, with once-quiet beaches such as Jimbaran beach now awash with seafood restaurants by the beach hawking everything from grilled fish and prawns to shellfish and even crabs and lobsters at reasonable prices. Diners select their desired seafood from tanks, which are then freshly grilled over a fire of coconut husks and served piping hot with a variety of spicy condiments. Tables on the beach allow diners to enjoy the cool sea breeze and a splendid view of the sunset in the evenings.

NASI PADANG

Originating from West Sumatra in Indonesia, Padang food is served in many areas in Bali. These eateries display a variety of dishes on plates stacked high in the windows, and customers are served dozens of small dishes ranging from beef *rendang* (a spicy coconut milk-based dry curry) to stewed vegetables and *sambal* seafood, together with steamed rice. Customers take what they want from the array and pay for their selection accordingly.

BABI GULING

This ceremonial roasted suckling pig dish is perhaps one of Bali's most well known dishes, and is typically served with a few slices of roast pork on top of rice and garnished with crispy pork skin. Traditional accompaniments include slices of fried pork sausage, pork sate (skewers) and most importantly, a fiery chilli sauce dip.

BEBEK OR AYAM BETUTU

This classic dish of roasted duck or chicken in banana leaf is a favourite with both locals and visitors. A mix of fiery spices and intense seasonings are rubbed on the poultry, which is then wrapped in betel nut leaves to seal in the flavours, and then slow-cooked for up to 10 hours. The result is tender, juicy meat that falls off the bone, with a spicy kick to round off the incredible flavour.

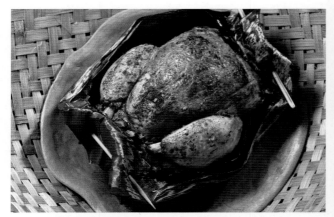

SATE LILIT

Balinese sate is made from a mixture of spices and finely chopped meat or seafood that is wrapped around a flat bamboo stick or twig of lemongrass. These richly flavoured skewers are grilled over hot charcoal until golden brown and slightly charred, and are best served with a creamy peanut sauce, or dipped in a mixture of salt and chopped chillies.

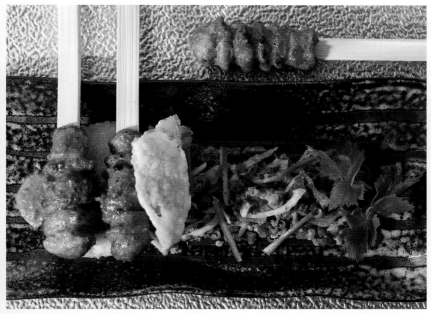

KOPI LUWAK

Also known as civet coffee, this prized drink is made from the beans of coffee berries that have been eaten and egested by the Asian palm civet, which lends them their distinctive flavour. Due to the labour-intensive method of harvesting the beans and its low-production rate, *kopi luwak* is the most expensive coffee in the world.

ARAK

This alcoholic spirit is made from the milky sap of sugarcane, palm or rice that is fermented and distilled, resulting in a clear liquid similar in taste to whisky and rum. Arak packs a heady alcoholic punch and is often combined with mixers such as lime juice, cola or soda water to make delicious cocktails.

SAMBAL KANGKUNG

TAHU ISI

A fragrant, moreish combination of water convolvulus stir-fried with spicy shrimp paste (*sambal*), *sambal kangkung* is commonly served alongside grilled seafood at many of Bali's beachfront restaurants.

This favourite childhood snack of fried tofu stuffed with a range of fillings from vegetables to minced meat and seafood is often served with a tasty chilli dip and can be found at many streetside stalls.

NASI CAMPUR

RUJAK

Often served at *warungs* (small casual cafes or shops), *nasi campur* consists of steamed rice topped with various side dishes from meat to fish and vegetables, topped off with a spoonful of *sambal* (spicy shrimp paste) or curry. This popular local dish is also sold as *nasi bungku*, packed in a conical banana leaf for easy takeaway.

One of Bali's most popular snacks is *rujak*, a mixture of crisp, unripe fruit and vegetables in sweet tamarind sauce that is commonly sold by pushcart vendors on the streets. Unripe mangoes, guavas, tubers and cucumbers are popular ingredients due to their crunchy, crisp texture, and the result is a fragrant, piquant snack when mixed with the tangy, spicy sauce.

JUKUT ARES

JAJA

Also known as chicken soup with banana stems, this traditional dish is made from the tender centre of young banana palms stewed with meat and spices. It is often served at Balinese ritual ceremonies and dished up for members of family and those who helped with the ceremonial arrangements.

A collective name for Balinese sweet snacks or cakes, *jaja* feature greatly in Balinese culture and are often served at important events such as a local wedding or tooth filing ceremony, as well as a casual snack for tea. Clockwise from left to right: *Kueh lapis* (layer cake); *Lak lak* (mini pancakes with sweet filling); *Jaja abug* (a traditional snack made from glutinous rice in coloured layers).

ABOUT THE PHOTOGRAPHER

Heinz von Holzen is a Swiss-born entrepreneur, chef, restaurateur, hotelier, adventurer and photographer. After moving to Singapore in 1980s to become a chef with the Hilton and Hyatt hotels, he discovered the art of food photography and has never looked back. In 1990, Heinz moved to Bali as the Executive Chef at the Grand Hyatt hotel, and later at the Ritz Carlton. After meeting Puji, his Balinese wife, Heinz further developed his passion for Indonesian cuisine and published nine cookbooks that he wrote and photographed over the years.

In his quest to record and discover even more Balinese dishes and recipes, Heinz travelled extensively to remote parts of the island, as well as to the peaks of numerous mountains and volcanoes. These journeys yielded many stunning images of Bali and its people, villages, scenery and everyday life that he now shares with you in this book.

Today, chef Heinz runs two authentic local restaurants in Bali, the multi-award-winning Bumbu Bali restaurant and cooking school, and Pasar Malam, a traditional market restaurant. He also runs Rumah Bali, a modern Balinese-style Bed & Breakfast in Tanjung Benoa at the southern tip of Bali.